G000024320

THE
LIONS
RUGBY
QUIZ BOOK

HOW MUCH DO YOU KNOW?

THE LIONS RUGBY QUIZ BOOK

HOW MUCH DO YOU KNOW?

MATTHEW JONES

y Lolfa

First impression: 2017

© Matthew Jones and Y Lolfa Cyf., 2017

Cover design: Y Lolfa

ISBN: 978 1 78461 373 0

Published and printed in Wales
on paper from well maintained forests by
Y Lolfa Cyf., Talybont, Ceredigion SY24 5HE
website www.ylolfa.com
e-mail ylolfa@ylolfa.com
tel 01970 832 304
fax 832 782

Introduction

The first international rugby tour occurred in 1882 when a team from Australia crossed the Tasman Sea to New Zealand. Six years later, cricketing entrepreneurs Arthur Shrewsbury and Alfred Shaw cobbled together a group of players from the British Isles. They set sail on 8 March 1888 for the Southern Hemisphere. These were to become the trailblazing forebears of today's modern-day British and Irish Lions. The tour established a blueprint that would be replicated in the years to come.

The British and Irish Lions are the most anticipated touring team in world rugby. This book is an opportunity for any rugby fan to test their knowledge on the events and personalities that have made the Lions such a cherished part of the sport. With 500 questions of varying difficulty, this has something for all.

Matthew Jones
February 2017

Round 1

1. **Who was named 'Man of the series' in the Lions' 2–1 test match victory over Australia in 2013?**
   a) Leigh Halfpenny
   b) Alun Wyn Jones
   c) Jonathan Sexton

2. **Who in 2009 became the 10th Irishman to captain a Lions touring squad?**
   a) Ronan O'Gara
   b) Donncha O'Callaghan
   c) Paul O'Connell

3. **In which year did the Lions first travel to their touring destination by aeroplane?**
   a) 1950
   b) 1955
   c) 1959

4. **Rory Underwood made seven appearances on the 1993 tour, while his younger brother Tony played in six matches. How many times did they play together?**
   a) 0
   b) 3
   c) 6

5. **Nairobi-born Simon Shaw made his Lions tour debut in 1997. In which year did he make his test debut for them?**

   a) 2001
   b) 2005
   c) 2009

6. **Alun Pask made eight test appearances for the Lions in the 1960s. Which club side did he play for?**

   a) Abertillery
   b) Ebbw Vale
   c) Newport

7. **Bangor centre Dick Milliken made 13 appearances on the 1974 tour. How many tries did he score?**

   a) 4
   b) 6
   c) 8

8. **Robert Jones played in all three tests of the 1989 tour of Australia. Who was the opposing scrum half for the test series?**

9. **Which member of the 1997 Lions squad was the first Scotland captain in the new professional era of rugby union?**

10. **Which Lions player in 1924 had a son of the same name who became a famous comedian and actor, known for roles in films such as *The Three Musketeers* and *Willy Wonka & the Chocolate Factory*?**

Round 2

1. **Welshmen Barry John, Phil Bennett and Malcolm Thomas all kicked the same number of conversions in a Lions shirt. How many did they each achieve?**

    a) 31

    b) 34

    c) 39

2. **New Zealand defeated the Lions 48–18 in the second test of the 2005 series. Who scored a record 33 points against the touring side?**

    a) Nick Evans

    b) Carlos Spencer

    c) Dan Carter

3. **Who was the only Scottish international to play in all six test matches of the 1997 and 2001 tours?**

    a) Gregor Townsend

    b) Alan Tait

    c) Tom Smith

4. **The Golden Lions lost 74–10 to the Lions in 2009. Which back-row forward collected the ball on his team's 22-metre line, before running the remaining length of the pitch to score a try?**

    a) Stephen Ferris

    b) Ryan Jones

    c) Tom Croft

5. **The 2001 Lions squad was the first to have a coach from outside the British Isles. Who was he?**

   a) Greg Smith

   b) Graham Henry

   c) Bernard Laporte

6. **In which year did Gus Black, Gordon Rimmer and Rex Willis all make test starts on tour?**

   a) 1950

   b) 1955

   c) 1959

7. **Who was the only ever-present Lion centre in the four-test series against South Africa in 1968?**

   a) Gerald Davies

   b) Jock Turner

   c) Barry Bresnihan

8. **Which three players were selected for both the 1989 and 1997 tours?**

9. **Who set a Lions record of 38 tries across two tours in the 1950s?**

10. **Pontnewydd-born Dai Parker landed ten conversions and five penalties on the 1930 tour, including a penalty from close to the halfway line in the final test against New Zealand. Which position did Parker play?**

Round 3

1. **Billy Whizz appeared in the comic *The Beano* for the first time in 1964. Which member of the 2001 Lions squad was nicknamed after this character?**
   a) Ben Cohen
   b) Jason Robinson
   c) Iain Balshaw

2. **Neil Jenkins started all three tests of the 1997 series. Which position did he play?**
   a) full back
   b) centre
   c) outside half

3. **Who was coach of the 1974 Lions squad?**
   a) Ken Smith
   b) Syd Millar
   c) Billy Cleaver

4. **Kelso-born wing Roger Baird scored 6 tries in 11 matches during the 1983 Lions tour. How many tries did he score in 27 Scotland test matches?**
   a) 0
   b) 6
   c) 14

5. **The 2005 tour kicked off with a home match in Cardiff. Who were the opposition?**
   a) France
   b) Samoa
   c) Argentina

6. **Lewis Jones broke a 46-year record for the most points scored in a Lions test during the first Australia test of 1950. Whose 11-point record did he break?**

    a) Jimmy Gillespie

    b) Percy Bush

    c) Gwyn Nicholls

7. **New South Wales lost 23–21 to the Lions in 1989. Who took advantage of a poor kick by David Campese and dummied his way through for a try?**

    a) Brendan Mullin

    b) Gavin Hastings

    c) Jeremy Guscott

8. **Which Bristol hooker made seven Lions test appearances across two tours in 1968 and 1971?**

9. **Which member of the 2001 Lions squad appeared in the BBC's 2013 series of *Strictly Come Dancing*?**

10. **The 2005 Lions tour consisted of 11 matches. Five different starting XV captains were used across these games. Who were they?**

Round 4

1. **Which of the following teams did Lions flanker Neil Back not play for?**
    a) Nottingham
    b) Leicester Tigers
    c) Orrell

2. **In which year did André Snyman, Henry Honiball and Ruben Kruger play against the Lions?**
    a) 1968
    b) 1974
    c) 1997

3. **Who scored all nine points for the Lions as they lost the fourth test against New Zealand at Eden Park in 1977?**
    a) Dougie Morgan
    b) Phil Bennett
    c) Andy Irvine

4. **Who formed the centre partnership with Brian O'Driscoll for the 2001 test series?**
    a) Scott Gibbs
    b) Rob Henderson
    c) Will Greenwood

5. **1997 Lions tourist Alan Tait earned 27 caps for Scotland. How many tries did he score for his country?**
    a) 8
    b) 13
    c) 17

6. **Who scored the only Lions try in the 14–14 drawn fourth test against the All Blacks in 1971?**

   a) Peter Dixon
   b) Gordon Brown
   c) David Duckham

7. **Who was the leading try-scoring forward for the Lions on the 1950 New Zealand and Australia tour, with 10 tries in 15 matches?**

   a) Don Hayward
   b) Karl Mullen
   c) Bill McKay

8. **Waikato defeated the Lions 38–10 in June 1993. Which future Lions coach scored a try for the Kiwi side in the game?**

9. ***Body Heat* was a game show aired by ITV from 1994 until 1996. Which Lions centre co-hosted the programme?**

10. **The Lions defeated South Western District 97–0 on the 1974 tour. Who scored six tries in the match?**

Round 5

1. **Which Welsh prop made five test appearances across the 2009 and 2013 Lions tours?**
   - a) Chris Horsman
   - b) Craig Mitchell
   - c) Adam Jones

2. **Who was voted 'Six Nations player of the championship' in 2004, a year before he was selected for his first Lions squad?**
   - a) Chris Cusiter
   - b) Gordon D'Arcy
   - c) Gavin Henson

3. **Hendon-born Chris Ralston made 13 appearances on the 1974 tour. Which position did he play?**
   - a) second row
   - b) number eight
   - c) hooker

4. **In 2002, who was voted Ireland's greatest-ever international?**
   - a) Jack Kyle
   - b) Mike Gibson
   - c) Willie John McBride

5. **Lancaster Park hosted an 11-point Lions victory against Canterbury in June 1971. Which forward received five fractures to his cheekbone during the game but still played to the final whistle?**

   a) Peter Dixon

   b) John Pullin

   c) Sandy Carmichael

6. **Jonny Wilkinson was selected for both the 2001 and 2005 Lions tours. With which club did he win the European Cup on two occasions?**

   a) Bayonne

   b) Toulon

   c) Clermont Auvergne

7. **Sam Walker captained the Lions on the 1938 tour of South Africa. Which club side did he play for?**

   a) Bective Rangers

   b) Queen's University

   c) Belfast Instonians

8. **Manawatu were defeated 109–6 by the Lions in 2005. Who scored five tries for the tourists in the match?**

9. **Which Lion won the 2011 BBC *Celebrity MasterChef* title?**

10. **Which two countries were represented in the make-up of the 1891 Lions squad?**

Round 6

1. **1891 Lions tour captain Bill Maclagan had retired from international rugby the previous year. What record had he set while playing for Scotland?**

   a) most-capped player in the world, with 25 appearances

   b) world-record try scorer, with 12 to his name

   c) the only person to have defeated England in ten consecutive matches

2. **Who was captain of the 1997 touring squad to South Africa?**

   a) Lawrence Dallaglio

   b) Keith Wood

   c) Martin Johnson

3. **Which back-row forward scored three tries from six matches on the 2001 tour of Australia?**

   a) Richard Hill

   b) Colin Charvis

   c) Martyn Williams

4. **Including replacements, how many players were selected for the 2005 touring squad to New Zealand?**

   a) 46

   b) 50

   c) 53

5. **What was the daily living expense paid to each member of the 1974 touring squad?**

    a) 75p
    b) £1.50
    c) £2.25

6. **David Irwin played at centre in the first, second and fourth tests of the 1983 tour. Who played out of position as his replacement in the third test?**

    a) John Rutherford
    b) Ollie Campbell
    c) Gwyn Evans

7. **Which Lion was president of the Lawn Tennis Association from 1962 until 1981?**

    a) Doug Prentice
    b) Vincent Griffiths
    c) Carl Aarvold

8. **Who was the only Irishman to start all three tests of the 2005 series against New Zealand?**

9. **Of the thirty players selected for the original 1966 Lions squad, eight shared the same profession. What was their role outside rugby?**

10. **Which future test series-winning Lions player and coach was born in Headingley on 30 October 1946?**

Round 7

1. **Which of the following scored the most points for the Lions?**

    a) Gareth Edwards

    b) Austin Healey

    c) Rob Andrew

2. **How many Lions matches did Willie John McBride play in over a five-tour career?**

    a) 65

    b) 70

    c) 82

3. **Ireland's Shane Horgan made eight appearances on the 2005 tour. How many games did he start?**

    a) 0

    b) 1

    c) 2

4. **Which back-row forward scored a try in his only Lions appearance on the 2001 tour of Australia?**

    a) Andy Ward

    b) Brett Sinkinson

    c) Simon Taylor

5. **In 1899, Gwyn Nicholls became the first Wales-based player to represent the Lions. Which club side did he play for?**

    a) Cardiff

    b) Glamorgan Wanderers

    c) Penarth

6. **The Brumbies beat the Lions 14–12 on the 2013 tour. Who coached the home side?**

    a) Mike Ruddock

    b) Eddie Jones

    c) Jake White

7. **Shane Williams scored two of the three Lions tries in the third test victory over South Africa in 2009. Who scored the other one?**

    a) Ugo Monye

    b) Riki Flutey

    c) Andrew Sheridan

8. **Who made two Lions test appearances on the 1997 Lions tour, nine years after his last England cap?**

9. **Which Newport player appeared in all 22 games of the 1903 tour, returning as top scorer with 59 points, including ten tries?**

10. **With five tries in five games, who was the Lions' top try scorer on the 1980 tour of South Africa?**

Round 8

1. **How many drop goals did Percy Bush, John Rutherford and Craig Chalmers achieve between them for the Lions?**

    a) 14

    b) 17

    c) 25

2. **Mike Catt was added to the 1997 Lions squad as an injury replacement. Whose thigh injury resulted in Catt's call-up?**

    a) Paul Grayson

    b) Arwel Thomas

    c) Eric Elwood

3. **The 2001 Lions lost three matches. Two were against Australia. Who were the other opposition to defeat them?**

    a) Western Australia

    b) Australia A

    c) New South Wales Country District

4. **While playing against Western Force, who was the only Lion to receive a yellow card on the 2013 tour?**

    a) Alun Wyn Jones

    b) Billy Twelvetrees

    c) Mako Vunipola

5. **Who in 1962 broke the record for most Lions appearances with a 42nd game on his third tour?**

   a) Bryn Meredith
   b) Arthur Smith
   c) Dickie Jeeps

6. **Taranaki lost by a 24-point margin to the Lions in June 1993. Which centre scored a brace of tries in the match?**

   a) Vince Cunningham
   b) Will Carling
   c) Scott Hastings

7. **David Lyons made a substitute appearance for Australia in the first Lions test of 2001. Which side did he join in 2008?**

   a) Ulster
   b) Glasgow Warriors
   c) Scarlets

8. **Broughton Park contributed a player to both the 1974 and 1977 tours. Who was he?**

9. **New Zealand defeated the Lions 18–17 in the first test of the 1959 tour. Who contributed all 18 points for the All Blacks?**

10. **Name the Irish outside half who started all three tests on the 2013 tour?**

Round 9

1. **Which of the following kicked the most conversions in a Lions jersey?**

    a) Andy Irvine
    b) Stephen Jones
    c) Bob Hiller

2. **Who scored a total of 108 tries in 327 matches from 1999 to 2014 for his province, country and Lions?**

    a) Denis Hickie
    b) Brian O'Driscoll
    c) Rob Henderson

3. **Dan Luger scored 24 tries in 38 England appearances. How many tries did he score in his two games on the 2001 Lions tour?**

    a) 4
    b) 5
    c) 6

4. **In which of the following years did the Lions lose to Otago, Auckland, Hawke's Bay and Waikato?**

    a) 1983
    b) 1993
    c) 2005

5. **Scotland's Iain Paxton scored four tries on the 1983 tour, making him the joint-top try-scoring forward. Which of his compatriots shared this achievement?**

    a) John Beattie
    b) Jim Calder
    c) Iain Milne

6. **Nigel Horton made four appearances on the 1977 tour. Which French side did he join in 1980?**

    a) Montauban
    b) Albi
    c) Saint-Claude

7. **Which Lion led the England cricket team that retained the Ashes in Australia during the 1894–95 season?**

    a) Tom Kent
    b) Andrew Stoddart
    c) Harry Speakman

8. **Who was the only Harlequins player selected for a Lions squad during the 1980s?**

9. **The Lions won the first test of the 1997 series in South Africa. Who scored 15 points for the tourists in the match?**

10. **Released in 2010, which Lion's autobiography was called *Raging Bull*?**

Round 10

1. **How many test tries did Willie Llewellyn, Jeff Butterfield and Alan Tait score in total for the Lions?**

    a) 6

    b) 8

    c) 11

2. **Which of the following hookers did <u>not</u> make a Lions test appearance in 2013?**

    a) Rory Best

    b) Richard Hibbard

    c) Tom Youngs

3. **Which scrum half found himself on the bench for the third test of the 2001 series, having been called up as a late replacement for Austin Healey?**

    a) Peter Stringer

    b) Bryan Redpath

    c) Andy Nicol

4. **Southland lost to the Lions in June 2005. Who bagged two tries in the game?**

    a) Lewis Moody

    b) Chris Cusiter

    c) Gavin Henson

5. **Who was New Zealand captain for the 1983 Lions series?**

   a) Murray Mexted
   b) Andy Dalton
   c) Andy Haden

6. **Who was the only uncapped member of the 1971 Lions squad?**

   a) Derek Quinnell
   b) Peter Dixon
   c) David Duckham

7. **Who were the two try scorers in the Lions' first test victory over New Zealand in 1930?**

   a) Jimmy Farrell and Brian Black
   b) Roger Spong and Paul Murray
   c) Jack Morley and James Reeve

8. **Which Scotland hooker, capped 32 times, was selected for both the 1966 and 1971 Lions squads?**

9. **Ronan O'Gara needed 11 stitches following a savage attack during the Lions' match against the Waratahs in 2001. Who perpetrated the aggression?**

10. **During the third test of the 1989 tour, who followed up a wayward drop-goal attempt from Rob Andrew, forcing David Campese into an error which resulted in a game-changing try?**

Round 11

1. Which of the following sides did <u>not</u> provide a player for the 1930 Lions squad?

   a) Old Millhillians

   b) Bradford

   c) Gloucester

2. The 1974 Lions had a 'call' which indicated that each player was to hit the closest opposition player to them. What was it?

   a) '99'

   b) a lion's roar

   c) 'old boys'

3. Nicknamed 'The Blackpool Tower', which English forward scored two tries in six matches on the 1989 tour?

   a) Paul Ackford

   b) Wade Dooley

   c) Dean Richards

4. The film *Rebecca's Daughters* starring Peter O'Toole was released in 1992. Which Lion, capped four times, played the role of Jonah in the film?

   a) Ray Gravell

   b) Roger Baird

   c) Ciaran Fitzgerald

5. **Western Australia lost by a 106-point margin to the Lions in 2001. Which scrum half scored two tries in the game?**

   a) Matt Dawson

   b) Austin Healey

   c) Rob Howley

6. **Which Englishman was a player on the 1891 Lions tour, captain of the 1896 tour and manager of the 1903 tour?**

   a) Matthew Mullineux

   b) Johnny Hammond

   c) Froude Hancock

7. **Who was the only Welsh representative on the inaugural Lions tour of 1888?**

   a) William Thomas

   b) Thomas Kent

   c) William Stadden

8. **Who captained the Lions to a 41–16 third test victory over Australia in 2013?**

9. **Lawrence Dallaglio was selected for three Lions tours. How many test matches did he play in?**

10. **Which member of the 2009 touring party graduated in veterinary medicine from the University of Glasgow in 2003?**

Round 12

1. In which year did Dawie de Villiers, Jan Ellis and Rodney Gould play against the Lions?

    a) 1962
    b) 1968
    c) 1974

2. How much was an official programme for New Zealand's third test against the Lions at Eden Park in July 1993?

    a) NZ$1
    b) NZ$3
    c) NZ$5

3. Who became the 800th player to wear a Lions jersey when he made his debut against the Queensland Reds in 2013?

    a) Sam Warburton
    b) Tom Youngs
    c) Sean Maitland

4. Who was the only non-Ireland-based Irishman in the 2009 squad?

    a) Stephen Ferris
    b) Tommy Bowe
    c) Jamie Heaslip

5. **Ben Kay made five appearances on the 2005 Lions tour. How many caps did he win for England?**

     a) 41
     b) 54
     c) 62

6. **Northern Free State lost 39–67 to the Lions in 1997. Which of the following backs scored a hat trick of tries in the match?**

     a) Tony Underwood
     b) Nick Beal
     c) John Bentley

7. **Ian McGeechan appeared in all eight Lions tests during the 1974 and 1977 tours. He started seven at centre but made one appearance as a substitute wing. Who did he replace?**

     a) Gareth Evans
     b) Elgan Rees
     c) J J Williams

8. **Which three players started at full back in the 2005 series against New Zealand?**

9. **Malcolm O'Kelly set an Irish record of 92 caps during his international career. How many Lions tours was he selected for?**

10. **The trophy competed for between Australia and the Lions, first raised in 2001, is named after which dual-nationality test player?**

Round 13

1. **Which of the following scored the most points in a Lions jersey?**
    a) Jonny Wilkinson
    b) Ollie Campbell
    c) Gordon Waddell

2. **Leeds-born Jason Robinson earned five Lions caps. How many Great Britain rugby league appearances did he make?**
    a) 12
    b) 15
    c) 18

3. **Scotsman James Robson held which role on the 2005 tour of New Zealand?**
    a) kicking coach
    b) head doctor
    c) media liaison officer

4. **Who was the ever-present scrum half for the Lions' 2009 test series against South Africa?**
    a) Chris Cusiter
    b) Dwayne Peel
    c) Mike Phillips

5. **Australia lost 13–29 in the first test of the 2001 Lions series. Who scored the visitors' first test try of the tour?**

   a) Dafydd James
   b) Rob Henderson
   c) Keith Wood

6. **Parc des Princes was the venue for a 29–27 Lions victory over France in 1989. Who captained the side?**

   a) Rob Andrew
   b) Gavin Hastings
   c) Phillip Matthews

7. **Who made his All Blacks debut at outside half in the first Lions test of the 1971 series?**

   a) Blair Furlong
   b) John Dougan
   c) Bob Burgess

8. **Whose autobiography, published in 1980, was called *Dai for England*?**

9. **Which Durham county cricketer scored 37 points in his first five Lions tour matches in 1962?**

10. **Which six members of the 1997 Lions squad were in England's starting XV when they won the 2003 Rugby World Cup final 20–17 against Australia?**

Round 14

1. **The New Zealand Rugby Union announced the ticket prices for the 2017 Lions tour in June 2016. How much was the most expensive ticket available?**

    a) NZ$349

    b) NZ$449

    c) NZ$599

2. **Which Lion was 'Six Nations player of the tournament' in 2006, 2007 and 2008?**

    a) Brian O'Driscoll

    b) Shane Williams

    c) Jonny Wilkinson

3. **The Lions defeated Western Australia in the first game of the 2001 tour. Which of the following did not score a hat trick of tries in the match?**

    a) Scott Quinnell

    b) Dan Luger

    c) Gordon Bulloch

4. **The Lions defeated a Marlborough-Nelson side 31–12 in June 1971. Which of the following scored a hat trick of tries in the game?**

    a) Chris Rea

    b) John Spencer

    c) Alastair Biggar

5. **John Carleton scored 48 points in 21 Lions matches across the 1980 and 1983 tours. Which club did he play for?**

   a) Moseley
   b) Orrell
   c) Sale

6. **Who replaced the injured Robin Thompson as Lions captain for the third test against South Africa in 1955?**

   a) Tom Reid
   b) Jeff Butterfield
   c) Cliff Morgan

7. **New Zealand defeated the Lions 16–12 in the first test of the 1977 series. Who scored a try following a 50-metre run in his 15th and final international?**

   a) Bill Osborne
   b) Grant Batty
   c) Bryan Williams

8. **Wagga Wagga-born Nathan Hines made five appearances on the 2009 tour. He was the only player in the squad based in which country?**

9. **Who made five appearances on the 2005 Lions tour, which was the equivalent to the total number of caps he gained for his country?**

10. **Which three-times Lions tourist played over 600 games for Pontypool between 1969 and 1992?**

Round 15

1. **Ten Welshmen appeared in the Lions starting XV for the third test against Australia in 2013. When was the last occasion for so many from that nation to appear together in a Lions test jersey?**

    a) 1950

    b) 1968

    c) 1974

2. **Ireland flanker Simon Easterby became the son-in-law of which fellow Lion in 2005?**

    a) Fergus Slattery

    b) Mike Burton

    c) Elgan Rees

3. **The Lions won 97–0 on 29 May 1974. Who were the opposition?**

    a) Griqualand West

    b) South Western Districts

    c) Rhodesia

4. **Mike Blair made three appearances on the 2009 tour. Whose broken ankle resulted in the Scotland captain being called into the squad?**

    a) Tomas O'Leary

    b) Danny Care

    c) Chris Cusiter

5. **Due to a mounting injury list, which Wallaby played as a centre for 35 minutes of the Lions' first test victory over Australia in 2013?**

   a) Michael Hooper
   b) Ben Mowen
   c) George Smith

6. **Who was New Zealand captain when they lost the 1971 series with the Lions 2–1?**

   a) Sid Going
   b) Ian Kirkpatrick
   c) Colin Meads

7. **Which of the following Lions made the most test appearances for Ireland?**

   a) Noel Murphy
   b) Jimmy Nelson
   c) Andy Mulligan

8. **Who scored 281 points in 43 Lions matches across three tours from 1974 to 1980?**

9. **Which Lion joined the Newcastle Falcons as Director of Rugby in 2012?**

10. **Bristol-born Mark Regan played six matches on the 1997 tour. Which club paid a £100,000 transfer fee to his hometown club for his services in the same year?**

Round 16

1. **How many players, including replacements, were called into the 2001 Lions touring party?**

    a) 37
    b) 44
    c) 48

2. **Who was coach of the 1971 Lions squad?**

    a) Jim Greenwood
    b) Bill McKay
    c) Carwyn James

3. **Which member of the 2009 squad played for Wellington against the Lions four years previously?**

    a) Riki Flutey
    b) Ugo Monye
    c) Lee Mears

4. **Which of the following did not appear in a test match on the 2013 tour of Australia?**

    a) Owen Farrell
    b) Justin Tipuric
    c) Sean Maitland

5. **Who scored his only try in 30 Lions appearances during the 9–3 victory over New Zealand at Dunedin in 1971?**

   a) Delme Thomas

   b) Ian McLauchlan

   c) Stack Stevens

6. **Dublin-born Phil Orr made two Lions tours, in 1977 and 1980. He played his last game for Ireland in 1987, finishing as his country's most-decorated prop. How many Irish caps did he earn?**

   a) 52

   b) 58

   c) 65

7. **The Lions scored just two tries in four tests against New Zealand in 1983. Who were the try scorers?**

   a) Hugo MacNeill and Roy Laidlaw

   b) Jim Calder and David Irwin

   c) John Rutherford and Roger Baird

8. **Which tour did the fly-on-the-wall documentary *Living with Lions* cover?**

9. **Two Scotland players received Lions caps on the 2001 tour. Who were they?**

10. **Bridgend-born Rob Howley made eight Lions appearances across two tours. Which club did he win the European Cup with in 2004?**

Round 17

1. **Argentina drew 25–25 with the Lions in May 2005. When had the Lions last faced the Pumas?**
    - a) 1936
    - b) 1955
    - c) 1974

2. **Born in March 1964, who was the oldest member of the 1997 Lions squad?**
    - a) Ieuan Evans
    - b) Jeremy Guscott
    - c) Alan Tait

3. **Which two players were selected for both the 1983 and 1989 Lions tours?**
    - a) Staff Jones and Jim Calder
    - b) Robert Ackerman and Robert Jones
    - c) Robert Norster and Donal Lenihan

4. **Which club is associated with three-times Lions tourist Derek Quinnell?**
    - a) Swansea
    - b) Aberavon
    - c) Llanelli

5. **Which Lion in 2009 was a team captain on the BBC show** *Hole in the Wall*?

    a) Matt Dawson

    b) Austin Healey

    c) Will Greenwood

6. **Dover-born Rob Henderson scored four tries in six matches during the 2001 tour. Which of the following teams did he not play for?**

    a) Munster

    b) Gloucester

    c) Toulon

7. **Who in 1910 became the first to score a try in each of his first three Lions tests?**

    a) Frank Handford

    b) Tommy Smyth

    c) Jack Spoors

8. **Graham Rowntree made 12 appearances across two Lions tours. In which years were these tours?**

9. **Which two-time Lions tourist was appointed head coach of French side Stade Aurillacois in 2011?**

10. **Which Lions captain had a son, Jeremy, who made his Scotland debut against France in 1986?**

Round 18

1. **In which year were Keith Savage, Derrick Grant and Gary Prothero selected together for a Lions squad?**

    a) 1966
    b) 1968
    c) 1971

2. **Leigh Halfpenny set a Lions test points-scoring record during the third match of the 2013 series. How many points did he achieve?**

    a) 21
    b) 23
    c) 26

3. **Shane Williams made 14 appearances over three Lions tours. In September 2016 he came out of retirement to play in Wales' Division 3 West B. Which club did he represent?**

    a) Llandeilo
    b) Amman United
    c) Burry Port

4. **Which member of the 2005 Lions squad appeared in the 2014-released comedy *Mrs Brown's Boys D'Movie*?**

    a) Malcolm O'Kelly
    b) John Hayes
    c) Shane Byrne

5. **Which two stadiums were used three times each during the 1974 tour of South Africa?**

    a) Newlands and Ellis Park
    b) Boland Stadium and Loftus Versfeld
    c) Free State Stadium and Boet Erasmus Stadium

6. **Who formed the second-row partnership for the first Lions test against New Zealand in 1977?**

    a) Bill Beaumont and Moss Keane
    b) Bill Beaumont and Gordon Brown
    c) Allan Martin and Moss Keane

7. **Who scored two tries on his New Zealand test debut as the All Blacks defeated the Lions 11–8 at Wellington in 1959?**

    a) Ralph Caulton
    b) Frank McMullen
    c) Don Clarke

8. **Which member of the 2001 Lions squad was temporarily head coach for Wales in 2009, while Warren Gatland was on Lions duty in South Africa?**

9. **Who was the only Irishman to appear in all four tests of the 1977 tour of New Zealand?**

10. **Paul Dodge made five appearances on the 1980 tour. Which club did he serve as player, backs coach and president?**

Round 19

1. Which of the following cities did <u>not</u> host a test match during the 1989 Lions tour of Australia?

    a) Brisbane
    b) Sydney
    c) Melbourne

2. Who was withdrawn from the 2013 Lions squad the day before departure for Australia, due to a suspension following his dismissal in the English Premiership final?

    a) Dylan Hartley
    b) Chris Ashton
    c) Tom Wood

3. Chris Cusiter made six appearances on the 2005 tour. Which club had he helped to win the Scottish Premiership title two years previously?

    a) Boroughmuir
    b) Hawick
    c) Glasgow Hawks

4. Which of the following Lions captained his home nation to victories over New Zealand, Australia and South Africa?

    a) Brian O'Driscoll
    b) John Pullin
    c) Ieuan Evans

5. **Which three-times capped Lion became the first permanent paid Secretary of the International Rugby Board in 1988?**

    a) Gordon Connell
    b) Ronnie Cowan
    c) Keith Rowlands

6. **Kevin Sinfield became Leeds rugby league club's highest points-scorer of all time in 2012. Whose 2,920-point, 48-year record did he break?**

    a) Gordon Rimmer
    b) Lewis Jones
    c) John Robins

7. **Who was the only player on the 1930 tour to make his Lions debut prior to his national bow?**

    a) George Beamish
    b) Jimmy Farrell
    c) John Hodgson

8. **Who was New Zealand captain for the 1977 test series against the Lions?**

9. **Which three-times Lions tourist managed the England national side from 2008 to 2011?**

10. **Three clubs provided four players each to the 1993 Lions squad. Harlequins and Bath were two of those clubs. Which was the third?**

Round 20

1. **Bath's Gareth Chilcott made five appearances on the 1989 tour. Which position did he play?**

   a) prop

   b) second row

   c) flanker

2. **Workington-born Mark Cueto made five Lions appearances on the 2005 tour. Which club did he represent on 303 occasions?**

   a) Leicester Tigers

   b) Newcastle Falcons

   c) Sale Sharks

3. **Who starred in the 2011 Channel 5 series *The Bachelor UK*?**

   a) Gavin Henson

   b) Shane Horgan

   c) Ugo Monye

4. **The Lions lost the first match of the 1971 tour 15–11. Who were the opposition?**

   a) Queensland

   b) New South Wales

   c) Waikato

5. Which scrum half scored a brace of tries for the Lions against the Barbarians in 2013?

    a) Ben Youngs
    b) Mike Phillips
    c) Eoin Reddan

6. Newcastle-born Steve Bainbridge made 11 appearances on the 1983 tour. As a talented junior athlete, which discipline did he hold a British colleges record in?

    a) shot put
    b) high jump
    c) javelin

7. Who played in every scrum position during the 1910 tour, scoring five tries in 18 matches?

    a) Robert Stevenson
    b) Oliver Piper
    c) Tommy Smyth

8. Donncha O'Callaghan made four Lions test appearances across two tours in 2005 and 2009. Which three countries did he play against?

9. How many times was Lewis Moody selected for a Lions tour?

10. The Ospreys won their first piece of silverware in 2005 when they lifted the Celtic League trophy. Which member of the 1997 Lions touring party captained the side to glory?

Round 21

1. **Duncan Macrae, Tom Elliot and Stan Coughtrie made a combination of 21 Lions appearances. Which country did they represent?**

   a) Ireland

   b) Scotland

   c) England

2. **In which year were Bob Hiller, Barry Bresnihan and Jock Turner selected together for a Lions tour?**

   a) 1968

   b) 1971

   c) 1974

3. **Born in September 1975, who was the youngest member of the 1997 Lions squad?**

   a) Austin Healey

   b) Matt Dawson

   c) Eric Miller

4. ***The Head Of Gonzo Davies* is a novel published in 2014. Which 1983 Lions tourist is the author?**

   a) Gwyn Evans

   b) Ian Stephens

   c) Eddie Butler

5. **The Lions defeated a SARA XV side 28–6 in May 1980. Which back-row forward scored two tries in the game?**

   a) John O'Driscoll
   b) Derek Quinnell
   c) Jeff Squire

6. **Who scored 18 tries in 14 matches during the 1971 tour?**

   a) David Duckham
   b) John Bevan
   c) Gareth Edwards

7. **Who scored 72 points, including 12 tries, from 22 appearances on the 1959 tour?**

   a) Bill Patterson
   b) David Hewitt
   c) Ken Scotland

8. **Which outside half broke his collarbone during the first test of the 1968 series against South Africa, ending his tour?**

9. **Who scored two tries for the home side in the Lions' two-point victory over Australia in the first test of the 2013 tour?**

10. **Who was the Lions' tour manager for the 2005 series in New Zealand?**

Round 22

1. **Who travelled on five consecutive Lions tours from 1966 to 1977?**
   a) Jim Telfer
   b) Gareth Edwards
   c) Mike Gibson

2. **The Barbarians defeated New Zealand 23–11 at Cardiff in 1973. Which Lions international captained the victorious side?**
   a) John Dawes
   b) John Pullin
   c) Fergus Slattery

3. **Which of the following coaches was not part of the Lions management team for the 2005 tour of New Zealand?**
   a) Ian McGeechan
   b) Gareth Jenkins
   c) Declan Kidney

4. **The Lions defeated Western Province 26–23 at Newlands on the 2009 tour. Who kicked a penalty with three minutes left on the clock to achieve the victory?**
   a) Ronan O'Gara
   b) James Hook
   c) Stephen Jones

5. **Who kicked eight points on his All Blacks debut in the third Lions test of the 1977 series?**
   a) Richard Wilson
   b) Brian McKechnie
   c) Bevan Wilson

6. **Which member of the 2001 Lions squad had a father called Ivor who was a member of the Newport team that defeated South Africa in 1969?**
   a) Mark Taylor
   b) Rob Howley
   c) Dai Young

7. **'The Bear' was a nickname given to which 1983 tourist due to his size and strength?**
   a) Donal Lenihan
   b) Maurice Colclough
   c) Iain Milne

8. **The Springbok squad came out for the third 2009 Lions test wearing armbands with the message 'Justice 4'. Which player's suspension was this referring to?**

9. **Who made eight consecutive test appearances at number eight for the Lions during the 1971 and 1974 tours?**

10. **Dickie Jeeps made nine test appearances for the Lions during the 1950s while playing for which English club side?**

Round 23

1. **How many Englishmen were in the Lions' starting line-up for the first New Zealand test in 2005?**

    a) 8
    b) 9
    c) 11

2. **Which club provided two full backs for the 2001 Lions squad?**

    a) Saracens
    b) Bath
    c) Northampton

3. **Scotland international Alan Tait made six appearances on the 1997 tour. Which of these rugby league teams did he not play for?**

    a) Widnes
    b) Leeds
    c) Wigan

4. **South Africa defeated the Lions 26–22 at Cape Town in the first test of the 1980 series. Which outside half scored 18 points in the match?**

    a) Ollie Campbell
    b) Tony Ward
    c) Gareth Davies

5. **David Rollo toured South Africa with the Lions in 1962. Which club did he represent until he was 40?**

   a) Greenock Wanderers
   b) Falkirk
   c) Howe of Fife

6. **Who earned as many Lions caps in 1977 as he did for his country throughout his career?**

   a) Brynmor Williams
   b) Nigel Horton
   c) Dougie Morgan

7. **England won the 2002 Hong Kong Sevens Cup by defeating Fiji 33–20 in the final. Which of the following 2005 Lions tourists was a member of the squad?**

   a) Charlie Hodgson
   b) Neil Back
   c) Josh Lewsey

8. **Who in 2009 became the youngest Welshman since Keith Jarrett in 1968 to be selected for a Lions squad?**

9. **Simon Taylor smashed his knee in the first game of the 2001 tour. Who was selected as his replacement?**

10. **Who started all three tests at scrum half for the Lions against New Zealand in 2005?**

Round 24

1. **In which year did Andy and Owen Farrell make history by being the first father-and-son combination to tour together with the Lions?**

   a) 2005
   b) 2009
   c) 2013

2. **Limerick-born John Moloney made eight appearances on the 1974 tour. Which position did he play?**

   a) scrum half
   b) outside half
   c) centre

3. **Who cut short his holiday in Tobago to join the 1997 Lions tour as a replacement for Rob Howley?**

   a) Kyran Bracken
   b) Rupert Moon
   c) Niall Hogan

4. **Andy Powell made five appearances on the 2009 tour of South Africa. Which rugby club did he join in 2015?**

   a) Bedford Blues
   b) Merthyr
   c) Old Belvedere

5. **Australia defeated the Lions 29–23 in the third test of the 2001 series. Who contributed 19 points to the Wallaby tally?**

   a) Stephen Larkham
   b) Elton Flatley
   c) Matt Burke

6. **Which club provided five players, including Wales international Teddy Morgan, to the 1904 touring party?**

   a) Birkenhead Park
   b) Hull and East Riding
   c) Guy's Hospital

7. **Who was the only player to start six matches on the 2013 tour?**

   a) Jonathan Davies
   b) Richie Gray
   c) Sean O'Brien

8. **Which dual-code international made his single Lions test appearance as a replacement for Jeremy Guscott in the third test of the 1997 series?**

9. **Michael Kiernan made his Lions test debut in 1983. Who was his five-times capped Lions international uncle?**

10. **Karl Mullen was captain of the 1950 Lions squad, leading the team in three tests. Who captained the team in the other three international matches?**

Round 25

1. **How many English Premiership titles did Ireland and Lions full back Geordan Murphy win during his Leicester playing career?**

   a) 5

   b) 8

   c) 10

2. **Which member of the 2005 Lions squad was nicknamed 'Mad Dog'?**

   a) Gordon Bulloch

   b) John Hayes

   c) Lewis Moody

3. **Who finished the second test of the 2009 tour as the Lions' centre partnership?**

   a) Stephen Jones and Tommy Bowe

   b) Ronan O'Gara and Luke Fitzgerald

   c) James Hook and Keith Earls

4. **Scotland scrum half Dougie Morgan played his entire career for which club side?**

   a) Stewart's Melville

   b) Howe of Fife

   c) Jed-Forest

5. As a result of his stance on apartheid in South Africa, which Lion never played for the Barbarians, due to him being considered a communist by their President, Brigadier Glyn Hughes?

    a) Billy Steele
    b) Roger Uttley
    c) John Taylor

6. Who scored the only try of the game as the Lions defeated New Zealand by six points in the first test of the 1971 tour at Dunedin?

    a) Mike Gibson
    b) Ian McLauchlan
    c) Sean Lynch

7. Who captained the 1930 tour of Australia and New Zealand?

    a) Jack Bassett
    b) Doug Prentice
    c) Harry Bowcott

8. Mike Phillips made his Lions debut against a Royal XV in May 2009. Which English side did he join in 2016?

9. Who set an eight-try record for a visiting forward on the 1974 tour of South Africa?

10. Who was the Bridgend prop who made five appearances on the 1980 tour before making his Wales bow a year later?

Round 26

1. **Which of the following cities did <u>not</u> host a test match during the 1983 tour of New Zealand?**
    - a) Christchurch
    - b) Hamilton
    - c) Dunedin

2. **Who was the only second row to start all three tests of the 1993 tour?**
    - a) Martin Bayfield
    - b) Martin Johnson
    - c) Andy Reed

3. **Which member of the 2001 Lions squad sang as a youthful choirboy at composer Andrew Lloyd Webber's wedding?**
    - a) Gordon Bulloch
    - b) Martin Corry
    - c) Lawrence Dallaglio

4. **ACT Brumbies lost by two points to the Lions in 2001 due to a last-gasp try by Austin Healey. Who converted the try to give the tourists victory?**
    - a) Ronan O'Gara
    - b) Matt Dawson
    - c) Jonny Wilkinson

5. **Ellis Park was the venue for the Lions' six-point victory over Gauteng Lions in 1997. Who scored an 80 m solo try, beating eight tacklers in the process?**

   a) Nick Beal
   b) Tim Stimpson
   c) John Bentley

6. **Who captained Australia to a 2–1 test series loss to the Lions in 2013?**

   a) Will Genia
   b) George Smith
   c) James Horwill

7. **The 1891 touring team won all 20 matches in South Africa including a test series whitewash. They only conceded one point on the entire tour. Who did they concede the point against?**

   a) Port Elizabeth
   b) Cape Town Clubs
   c) Eastern Province

8. **Which pacy winger and member of the 1989 Lions squad inspired a new tradition for England fans in 1988 when they first started to sing 'Swing Low, Sweet Chariot'?**

9. **Who set a front-row record of 12 consecutive Lions test appearances from 1977 to 1983?**

10. **Who were the three scrum halves to be capped by the Lions on the 1968 tour of South Africa?**

Round 27

1. **Who was named in September 2016 as head coach for the following year's Lions tour to New Zealand?**
   - a) Scott Johnson
   - b) Warren Gatland
   - c) Vern Cotter

2. **Iain Balshaw made eight appearances on the 2001 tour, scoring two tries. Which of the following sides did he <u>not</u> play for?**
   - a) Munster
   - b) Gloucester
   - c) Biarritz Olympique

3. **Which of the following players scored the most points for the Lions?**
   - a) Terry Davies
   - b) Mike Gibson
   - c) Tim Stimpson

4. **Australia defeated the Lions 30–12 in the first test of the 1989 series. Who formed the centre partnership in the match?**
   - a) Mike Hall and Brendan Mullin
   - b) Jeremy Guscott and Will Carling
   - c) Scott Hastings and John Devereux

5. **Who was the starting scrum half in the Lions' first match of the 2005 tour at home in Cardiff?**

    a) Peter Stringer
    b) Gareth Cooper
    c) Mike Blair

6. **Who in 1966 against the Wallabies set a Lions record of five conversions in a test match?**

    a) David Watkins
    b) Don Rutherford
    c) Stewart Wilson

7. **Which Scottish centre made his Lions debut in 1924, two years before winning three caps for his country?**

    a) Alpin Thomson
    b) Ernest Fahmy
    c) Roy Kinnear

8. **Who came out of international retirement to make a single Lions appearance on the 2013 tour against the ACT Brumbies?**

9. **Which member of the 2005 Lions squad was named 'Scotland player of the year' the following season?**

10. **England's Dorian West was called up as a replacement for the 2001 squad to Australia. What was his job before becoming a professional rugby player?**

Round 28

1. **Ireland internationals Mick English, Noel Murphy and Gordon Wood made 54 Lions appearances between them. In which year were they selected for the same touring party?**
    a) 1959
    b) 1962
    c) 1966

2. **Brisbane-born Tom Court made his Lions debut against Melbourne Rebels in 2013. Which country did he represent for the first time in 2009?**
    a) Scotland
    b) Ireland
    c) Wales

3. **Which of the following made the most appearances on the 2005 tour?**
    a) John Hayes
    b) Danny Grewcock
    c) Gethin Jenkins

4. **South Africa won the second 2009 test by three points. Which of their players was yellow carded in the match for attempting to gouge Luke Fitzgerald?**
    a) Schalk Burger
    b) Bakkies Botha
    c) Bismarck du Plessis

5. **Colin Charvis made 94 test appearances for Wales and two for the Lions. Where was he born?**

   a) Sutton Coldfield

   b) Limerick

   c) Dundee

6. **The 1971 Lions squad contained a record-equalling seven players from the same club, London Welsh. Which club had provided seven players in 1910?**

   a) Watsonians

   b) Bristol

   c) Newport

7. **Which Englishman managed the 1908 tour of New Zealand and Australia?**

   a) George Harnett

   b) Henry Speakman

   c) Jack Clowes

8. **Which former prop was scrum coach for the 2009 tour?**

9. **Which country supplied a hooker for every Lions tour from 1938 until 1966?**

10. **Who were the Scottish father and son who played in Lions tests during the 1924 and 1962 tours respectively?**

Round 29

1. **Geoff Parling made his Lions debut against Western Force in June 2013. Which position is he associated with?**

    a) full back
    b) centre
    c) second row

2. **Which of the following kicked the most conversions in his Lions career?**

    a) Neil Jenkins
    b) Ronan O'Gara
    c) Gavin Hastings

3. **Jeremy Davidson made 13 appearances across two tours for the Lions. How many caps did he win for Ireland?**

    a) 32
    b) 46
    c) 55

4. **Clive Rowlands was manager of the 1989 tour of Australia. Who were appointed as coaches for the trip?**

    a) John Dawes and Jim Telfer
    b) Ian McGeechan and Roger Uttley
    c) Mike Gibson and Andy Ripley

5. **How many tries did the Lions score in the 22 matches of the 1974 tour?**

    a) 93
    b) 107
    c) 119

6. **Who was the only Welsh prop to make a test appearance on the 2001 tour, when he came off the bench in the final decisive encounter with Australia?**

    a) Ben Evans
    b) Dai Young
    c) Darren Morris

7. **The first ever Lions match was against Otago on 28 April 1888. Which club contributed four players for the game?**

    a) Swinton
    b) Batley
    c) Runcorn

8. **Jason Leonard made five test appearances for the Lions from 1993 to 2001. Which club side did he represent on 290 occasions, spanning both the amateur and professional era?**

9. **Who scored a brace of tries for New Zealand as they beat the Lions 38–19 in the third test of the 2005 series?**

10. **Why was the 1908 touring squad an Anglo-Welsh affair?**

Round 30

1. **Who in 2001 became the first person to captain two Lions tours?**

    a) Martin Johnson

    b) Keith Wood

    c) Richard Hill

2. **How many tries did the Lions score against Manawatu on the 2005 tour?**

    a) 11

    b) 14

    c) 17

3. **During the 2001 tour, which Australian forward did Austin Healey refer to as a 'plank'?**

    a) John Eales

    b) Matt Cockbain

    c) Justin Harrison

4. **In 1888, Arthur Paul became the first Lions tourist from which country?**

    a) Scotland

    b) Ireland

    c) England

5. Australia lost by a point to the Lions in the second test of the 1989 tour. There were several controversial incidents during a bad-tempered encounter. Who aimed a kick towards Steve Cutler's head at the side of a ruck just before half-time?

    a) David Sole
    b) Dai Young
    c) Mike Teague

6. Scotland centre Chris Rea scored three tries in ten tour matches during 1971. Which English club did he represent?

    a) Headingley
    b) Harlequins
    c) Richmond

7. Which member of the 1950 touring party was captain of the British track and field team at the 1954 European Athletics Championships?

    a) Ivor Preece
    b) Ranald MacDonald
    c) Ken Jones

8. Flanker Simon Easterby made five appearances on the 2005 tour. Which side was he head coach of before becoming Ireland's forwards coach in 2014?

9. The Lions defeated a West Coast-Buller side 39–6 at Greymouth in June 1971. Who scored six tries in the match?

10. The Lions defeated Western Australia by 57 points in the first match of the 1966 tour. Which prop landed three conversions in the match?

Round 31

1. In which year did British newspapers first send journalists abroad to cover a full Lions tour?

    a) 1950

    b) 1955

    c) 1959

2. Brian Moore made 14 appearances across the 1989 and 1993 tours. Which position did he play?

    a) hooker

    b) flanker

    c) wing

3. Which ground formed the backdrop for the final Lions test of the 1974 tour, a 13–13 draw with South Africa?

    a) Loftus Versfeld

    b) Van Riebeeck Stadium

    c) Ellis Park

4. Who scored a brace of tries as the Lions lost the second 1971 test to the All Blacks 22–12 at Christchurch?

    a) David Duckham

    b) Gerald Davies

    c) Mike Gibson

5. Which of the following achievements did Brian O'Driscoll not achieve during his playing career?

    a) two Six Nations Grand Slams

    b) three European Cups

    c) four Celtic League titles

6. **Of the 42 tries scored by the Lions on the 2013 tour, how many were achieved by Welshmen?**

    a) 12
    b) 18
    c) 20

7. **Tom Kent scored the first ever try by a Lions player, on the 1888 tour. Which club did he play for?**

    a) Blackheath
    b) Salford
    c) Batley

8. **Martyn Williams was capped 100 times for Wales and selected for three Lions tours. How many Lions caps did he win?**

9. **Which scrum half made his only Lions test appearance as a 55th-minute replacement for Riki Flutey in the third international of the 2009 tour?**

10. **John Jackett and James Davey were both selected for the 1908 Lions tour. What else did they achieve in the same year?**

Round 32

1. **Gordon Connell, Billy Steele and Iain Milne made a total of 20 appearances between them for the Lions. Which country did they play for?**
   a) Scotland
   b) England
   c) Ireland

2. **How much was an official programme for South Africa's fourth test against the Lions in September 1955?**
   a) one shilling
   b) three shillings
   c) five shillings

3. **Which of the following scored the most points in a Lions jersey?**
   a) Matt Dawson
   b) David Watkins
   c) Craig Chalmers

4. **Ryan Jones made a try-scoring debut on the 2005 tour. Who were the opposition?**
   a) Southland
   b) Otago
   c) New Zealand

5. The Lions won the first 2013 test against Australia by two points. Who missed a kickable penalty on the final whistle to allow the tourists a victory?

    a) Christian Leali'ifano
    b) James O'Connor
    c) Kurtley Beale

6. Tony Stanger made a single appearance on the 1997 tour against Northern Free State. Which French side did he join in 1999?

    a) Dax
    b) Grenoble
    c) Brive

7. Who in 1938 kicked three gigantic penalties while setting a Lions points record during the first test against South Africa?

    a) Jeff Reynolds
    b) Viv Jenkins
    c) Russell Taylor

8. Who was the ever-present New Zealand scrum half during the 1971 Lions test series?

9. During the 1980s, who became the first pair of twins to represent the Lions?

10. Rory Underwood scored seven tries from 17 Lions matches. Did his younger brother Tony score more or less?

Round 33

1. **There were four Irishmen in the 1997 Lions touring party. In which country did they all play their club rugby?**

    a) England

    b) France

    c) Italy

2. **Gavin Hastings played in all three test matches of the 1993 series. Who was the other full back in the squad?**

    a) Jon Webb

    b) Jim Staples

    c) Tony Clement

3. **Who was the Australian starting line-up scrum half in all three tests of the 2001 series?**

    a) George Gregan

    b) Chris Whitaker

    c) Matt Henjak

4. **Which England prop made 12 appearances across the 2005 and 2013 tours without earning a test cap?**

    a) Perry Freshwater

    b) Andrew Sheridan

    c) Matt Stevens

5. **Which of the following Lions who acted as captains on the BBC's *A Question Of Sport* had the longest run on the show?**

   a) Cliff Morgan
   b) Bill Beaumont
   c) Gareth Edwards

6. **Which Lions tourist was detained by Australian officials on entry into the country in 1971, due to the fact he'd answered the question 'Is it your intention to bring down the elected government of Australia?' with 'sole purpose of visit'?**

   a) Bob Hiller
   b) Derek Quinnell
   c) Ian McLauchlan

7. **What did Fenton Smith and Phil Waller both achieve on the 1910 tour?**

   a) played in 23 of the 24 tour matches
   b) scored a try in each of the three test matches
   c) won more caps for the Lions than for their country

8. **Whose 133rd test appearance in 2016 made him the most-capped front-row forward in world rugby?**

9. **Tyrone Howe made a single appearance on the 2001 Lions tour. Which Irish province did he represent on 100 occasions?**

10. **Who was the former Ireland forward who became manager of the 1980 tour of South Africa?**

Round 34

1. **In which year did the Lions adopt an all-red jersey for the first time?**
    - a) 1950
    - b) 1962
    - c) 1968

2. **Scotland number eight David MacMyn captained the 1927 touring party. Which country did they visit?**
    - a) Canada
    - b) Russia
    - c) Argentina

3. **Which of the following players was uncapped when selected for the 1997 Lions tour?**
    - a) Will Greenwood
    - b) Tim Stimpson
    - c) Nick Beal

4. **Griqualand West faced the Lions in July 1980, losing by four points. Who scored a try and kicked a drop goal in the match?**
    - a) Mike Slemen
    - b) David Richards
    - c) John Robbie

5. **Australia lost by seven points to the Lions in the second test of the 1989 tour. Who were the two players that scored tries for the tourists in the match?**
   a) Gavin Hastings and Jeremy Guscott
   b) Mike Teague and Rory Underwood
   c) David Sole and Ieuan Evans

6. **Who scored ten tries in seven matches during the 2001 tour?**
   a) Brian O'Driscoll
   b) Jason Robinson
   c) Dafydd James

7. **Alan Morley made two appearances on the 1974 tour. What record did he set when his career came to an end?**
   a) a world record 479 tries scored in first-class rugby
   b) first England international to score a try in seven consecutive matches
   c) 100% win record as England captain, with four wins in four games

8. **Which Ireland international captained the 1959 Lions party to Australia and New Zealand?**

9. **Rotorua hosted the first Lions match on New Zealand soil in 2005, with the visitors winning by a margin of 14 points. Who were the opposition?**

10. **Who were the two players selected for both the 1977 and 1983 tours?**

Round 35

1. **Steve Boyle, Colin Deans and Trevor Ringland made a combined 24 appearances for the Lions. In which year were they selected for the same touring squad?**

    a) 1977
    b) 1980
    c) 1983

2. **Who scored 35 points from six matches on the 2009 tour of South Africa?**

    a) James Hook
    b) Phil Godman
    c) Toby Flood

3. **British Prime Minister Tony Blair phoned the Lions captain prior to the 2005 encounter with the Hurricanes to wish the team his best. Who took the call and responded with 'Tony who?'?**

    a) Gareth Thomas
    b) Brian O'Driscoll
    c) Paul O'Connell

4. **Who was South Africa's losing captain in the 1997 series against the Lions?**

    a) André Joubert
    b) Mark Andrews
    c) Gary Teichmann

5. **In which year were André Watson, Jonathan Kaplan and Paddy O'Brien used as referees for a Lions series?**

   a) 1993
   b) 1997
   c) 2001

6. **During the third test of the 1974 tour, which Lions forward punched Northern Transvaal forward Johan de Bruyn, sending his glass eye into the mud?**

   a) Bobby Windsor
   b) Gordon Brown
   c) Stewart McKinney

7. **Who opened the scoring with his first ever drop goal in the Lions' third test against South Africa at Pretoria in 1955?**

   a) Dickie Jeeps
   b) Doug Baker
   c) Jeff Butterfield

8. **Who became the first Lions kicking coach when appointed to the role for the 1997 tour?**

9. **Who formed a centre partnership with Brian O'Driscoll for the 2001 test series against Australia?**

10. **Carl Aarvold scored 20 tries in 26 Lions matches. Professionally, he was a barrister who became Recorder of London. Which famous trial did he preside over in 1965?**

Round 36

1. **Which Lions outside half scored 16 tries in 128 appearances for his country?**
    a) Neil Jenkins
    b) Ronan O'Gara
    c) Jonny Wilkinson

2. **Toutai Kefu was an ever-present starter for Australia during the 2001 test series with the Lions. Which position did he play?**
    a) second row
    b) flanker
    c) number eight

3. ***The Power of Four* was an anthem commissioned by Clive Woodward for the 2005 tour. Which Welsh singer was the first person to perform the song in public?**
    a) Katherine Jenkins
    b) Bryn Terfel
    c) James Dean Bradfield

4. **Rob Andrew arrived on the 1989 tour of Australia as an injury replacement. Whose trip ended with a knee injury in the first match, making way for the English outside half?**
    a) Stuart Barnes
    b) Jonathan Davies
    c) Paul Dean

5. **John Willcox was the highest points-scoring Lion in the 1962 test series. How many points did he achieve?**

    a) 5
    b) 7
    c) 8

6. **Who scored a brace of tries in both the second and third tests of the 1974 tour of South Africa?**

    a) J J Williams
    b) Ian McGeechan
    c) Billy Steele

7. **Jim Greenwood played in all four tests on the 1955 tour of South Africa. Which club did he play for?**

    a) Edinburgh Wanderers
    b) Hawick
    c) Dunfermline

8. **Which English club appointed Dai Young as Director of Rugby in 2011?**

9. **Which member of the 2001 Lions touring party had the nickname Nobby?**

10. **Prior to the Lions leaving for the 1974 tour to apartheid-era South Africa, who addressed the squad by saying 'Gentlemen, if you have any doubts about going on this tour, I want you to be big enough to stand up now and leave this room'?**

Round 37

1. **Which Lions squad was branded as 'the Invincibles'?**

    a) 1971
    b) 1974
    c) 1983

2. **Peter Winterbottom made seven Lions test appearances across two tours. Which ones?**

    a) 1980 and 1989
    b) 1983 and 1993
    c) 1989 and 1993

3. **Matt Perry played six matches on the 2001 tour. His 36 England appearances constituted a then-record for a full back. How old was he when he made his final appearance in an English jersey?**

    a) 24
    b) 31
    c) 36

4. **Which Lions forward was deprived of a match-winning try in the fourth test against South Africa in 1974, with the referee ruling he had not grounded the ball correctly?**

    a) Roger Uttley
    b) Fergus Slattery
    c) Ian McLauchlan

5. **Which Lions tourist appeared in a 2012 episode of *Celebrity Come Dine With Me* in Ireland?**

   a) Jeremy Davidson

   b) Gordon D'Arcy

   c) Shane Byrne

6. **Who was manager of the 1974 Lions touring party?**

   a) David Marques

   b) Hugh McLeod

   c) Alun Thomas

7. **Who scored 53 points in 11 matches on the 1980 tour of South Africa?**

   a) Andy Irvine

   b) Gareth Davies

   c) Clive Woodward

8. **Who came off the bench in the third test of the 2009 tour, making him the only Scotland international to take part in the test series?**

9. **Keith Wood started at hooker for the Lions in five of the six tests played during the 1997 and 2001 tours. Who was first-choice hooker in the remaining international?**

10. **In 1891, who became the first pair of brothers to play in a Lions international match together?**

Round 38

1. **Which of the following scored the most tries in a Lions shirt?**

   a) Andy Irvine

   b) Peter Jackson

   c) Arthur Smith

2. **Which Englishman was named manager of the 1993 Lions tour?**

   a) Geoff Cooke

   b) Richard Sharp

   c) Dick Greenwood

3. **Who were the joint-top Lions try scorers, with four each, on the 2013 tour of Australia?**

   a) Leigh Halfpenny and Brian O'Driscoll

   b) Jonathan Davies and Ben Youngs

   c) Alex Cuthbert and George North

4. **Whose Lions career consisted of a single match against a SARA XV side in May 1980, due to a rib injury cutting short his tour?**

   a) Alan Tomes

   b) Phil Blakeway

   c) Mike Rafter

5. **Tony Underwood scored a Lions hat trick on 1 July 1997. Who was this against?**

    a) Northern Free State

    b) Eastern Province

    c) Emerging Springboks

6. **Melrose forward Jim Telfer made his Lions debut in May 1966. In which year did he coach Scotland to their first Five Nations Grand Slam in 59 years?**

    a) 1980

    b) 1982

    c) 1984

7. **Zambia made its international debut in a match against a touring East Africa side in 1975. Which Lions second row represented the home side?**

    a) Bill Mulcahy

    b) Mike Campbell-Lamerton

    c) Peter Stagg

8. **Who in 1971 became the first Welshman to captain a Lions touring squad?**

9. **In 2005, Manawatu lost by a 103-point margin to the Lions. Who scored five tries in the game?**

10. **Galashiels-born Craig Chalmers made 60 test appearances for Scotland. How many Lions caps did he achieve?**

Round 39

1. **Mako Vunipola made his Lions debut in June 2013. Which country did he represent when he made his international debut in 2012?**

   a) Scotland
   b) England
   c) Ireland

2. **How many Englishmen, including replacements, were selected for the 1997 Lions touring party?**

   a) 19
   b) 22
   c) 24

3. **Whose 1993 tour was cut short after just three matches due to a shattered cheekbone?**

   a) Scott Hastings
   b) Ian Hunter
   c) Richard Webster

4. **Who were the two Welshmen that appeared in the Lions team which defeated France by two points in 1989?**

   a) Ieuan Evans and Robert Norster
   b) John Devereux and Tony Clement
   c) Robert Jones and Mike Griffiths

5. Which member of the 1980 and 1983 touring squads was born in Borneo on 27 November 1957?

   a) John Carleton
   b) Terry Holmes
   c) John Beattie

6. Brothers James and Joseph Wallace were both selected for the 1903 tour of South Africa. Which club did they play for?

   a) Malone
   b) Wanderers
   c) Lansdowne

7. Which member of the 2009 Lions squad had a father called Des who played 34 times for Ireland, and represented the Lions in 1986?

   a) Luke Fitzgerald
   b) Keith Earls
   c) Tommy Bowe

8. Who scored all of the Lions' points when they lost 16–15 to Australia in the second 2013 test match?

9. Who was the Fylde second row who was named Lions captain for the 1980 tour of South Africa?

10. Which Irish prop earned nine Lions caps over three tours in 1959, 1962 and 1968?

Round 40

1. **Denis Hickie scored 29 tries in 62 Ireland international appearances. How many tries did he score in five games on the 2005 Lions tour?**

    a) 0
    b) 2
    c) 5

2. **Which of the following started all three tests on the 2013 tour of Australia?**

    a) Geoff Parling
    b) Jamie Heaslip
    c) Adam Jones

3. **Which of the following Scotland props made the most Lions test appearances?**

    a) Ian McLauchlan
    b) Sandy Carmichael
    c) David Sole

4. **Who sparked a near-riot, with one fan going after him with a stick, after he caught Tommy Bedford with a right hook in the Lions match against Natal in 1974?**

    a) Andy Ripley
    b) Fergus Slattery
    c) J P R Williams

5. **South Africa won the third 1997 test 35–16. Who contributed 13 points to the Springboks' tally?**

    a) Percy Montgomery

    b) Jannie de Beer

    c) Theo van Rensburg

6. **Who were the two Lions try scorers in the 1993 test series?**

    a) Ieuan Evans and Nick Popplewell

    b) Rory Underwood and Scott Gibbs

    c) Gavin Hastings and Ben Clarke

7. **Which statistic links England internationals Jeff Butterfield and Jeremy Guscott?**

    a) scored tries on their international debuts for both country and Lions

    b) made ten consecutive Lions test appearances

    c) played for the Lions in four different positions

8. **Australia won the 2001 Lions series 2–1. Who captained the Wallabies?**

9. **Which Scotland forward who toured with the Lions in 1955 and 1959 made a record 40 consecutive appearances for his country between 1954 and 1962?**

10. **Who was the England rugby union international that made four Lions test appearances in 1959, before following in the footsteps of his Wales rugby league international father and changing codes in 1961 to represent Great Britain in the 13-man game?**

Round 41

1. Which of the following coaches was <u>not</u> part of the Lions' management team for the 2005 tour of New Zealand?

    a) Eddie O'Sullivan

    b) Lynn Howells

    c) Phil Larder

2. Jack Kyle scored seven tries in 20 Lions matches during the 1950 tour. Which position did he play?

    a) outside half

    b) wing

    c) full back

3. Orange Free State lost by a 22-point margin to the Lions in 1997. Which of the following wingers scored a hat trick of tries in the game?

    a) John Bentley

    b) Tony Underwood

    c) Ieuan Evans

4. Which of these clubs did Gerald Davies <u>not</u> represent?

    a) Cardiff

    b) London Welsh

    c) Ebbw Vale

5. **Who did Scotland second row Gordon Brown affectionately describe as 'the archetypal loveable rogue'?**

    a) Derek Quinnell

    b) Phil Orr

    c) Bobby Windsor

6. **Which New Zealand second row played in all eight test matches during the 1977 and 1983 Lions tours?**

    a) Frank Oliver

    b) Andy Haden

    c) Gary Whetton

7. **Australia defeated the Lions 35–14 in the second test of the 2001 tour. Which forward scored the tourists' only try of the match?**

    a) Neil Back

    b) Keith Wood

    c) Scott Quinnell

8. **Which member of the 1971 Lions team was dubbed 'The King' by the New Zealand press?**

9. **Which three members of the 1997 Lions squad were in England's starting XV at the 2007 Rugby World Cup final?**

10. **Following a clash of heads in training, which Scottish forward was incorrectly reported to have had a fight with John Hayes during the 2005 tour?**

Round 42

1. **Which was the first year for the Lions squad to consist entirely of players who already had international caps?**
   - a) 1938
   - b) 1950
   - c) 1959

2. **How many appearances did Christian Wade, Brad Barritt and Shane Williams make between them on the 2013 tour?**
   - a) 3
   - b) 4
   - c) 5

3. **Wigan-born Fran Cotton made 31 England international appearances from 1971 to 1981. How many Lions tests did he play in over three tours?**
   - a) 4
   - b) 7
   - c) 10

4. **Natal lost by 30 points to the Lions in June 1997. Which player's tour was ended in the match due to a dislocated shoulder?**
   - a) Rob Howley
   - b) Gregor Townsend
   - c) Paul Wallace

5. **Which Lions tourist played his 87th and final match for Scotland in September 2007, ending his international career as his country's most-capped international?**

   a) Tom Smith
   b) Rob Wainwright
   c) Scott Murray

6. **New Zealand Maori defeated the Lions for the first time in their history in 2005. Who scored the home side's only try?**

   a) Marty Holah
   b) Jono Gibbes
   c) Leon MacDonald

7. **Colm Tucker made nine appearances on the 1980 tour. He was the first player from which club side to be selected for the Lions?**

   a) Shannon
   b) Dolphin
   c) Cork Constitution

8. **Who in 1993 set a Lions record of 38 points in a test series?**

9. **Robin McBryde was a 2001 Lions tourist. In 2007 he became the Bearer of the Grand Sword at the National Eisteddfod. Which fellow Lion had previously held this role?**

10. **Lawrence Dallaglio dislocated his ankle in the first half of the Lions match against Bay of Plenty in 2005. Who was the Ireland international that joined the tour as his replacement?**

Round 43

1. **Which position is associated with Cian Healy, Euan Murray and Julian White?**

   a) prop

   b) second row

   c) flanker

2. **Which member of the 2013 Lions squad scored a record-equalling four-try haul for the Crusaders in a 52–10 victory over the Brumbies in March 2011?**

   a) Manu Tuilagi

   b) Sean Maitland

   c) Rob Kearney

3. **Who was the Scottish prop that formed the ever-present Lions front-row with Brian Moore and Dai Young in the 1989 test series?**

   a) Gregor Mackenzie

   b) David Sole

   c) Paul Burnell

4. **David Richards made seven appearances on the 1980 tour. For which club did he score 112 tries in 305 appearances?**

   a) Cardiff

   b) Swansea

   c) Bridgend

5. **The Lions defeated a Wanganui-King Country side by 51 points in June 1977. Who scored five tries in the match?**

    a) Mike Gibson

    b) Andy Irvine

    c) David Burcher

6. **Which twice-capped Lion retired from England duty in 1969 as his country's most-decorated international, having made 34 test appearances?**

    a) Tony Horton

    b) Richard Sharp

    c) Budge Rogers

7. **The Lions toured South Africa in 1962. Who was their Scottish captain?**

    a) David Rollo

    b) Gordon Waddell

    c) Arthur Smith

8. **Which four Lions started all three South Africa games in 2009?**

9. **Known as 'The Flying Prince', who scored 12 tries in six matches on the 1936 tour?**

10. **Did Dusty Hare, Gavin Hastings and Matt Perry make more Lions appearances between them than J P R Williams on his own?**

Round 44

1. **The Lions played 16 test matches over three tours in the 1950s. How many did they win?**

   a) 7

   b) 9

   c) 11

2. **Ian McGeechan was coach of the 1993 squad in New Zealand. Which Englishman acted as his assistant?**

   a) Roger Uttley

   b) Dick Best

   c) Peter Rossborough

3. **Rodger Arneil, Stack Stevens and Geoff Evans had what in common during the 1971 tour?**

   a) they were squad replacements

   b) they were the first Lion from their club side

   c) they played in 12 matches without making a test appearance

4. **Which of the following back-row forwards did <u>not</u> score a test try during the 2005 series against New Zealand?**

   a) Simon Easterby

   b) Lewis Moody

   c) Ryan Jones

5. **What tragic event happened on 15 July 1888, during the inaugural Lions tour?**

    a) 12 fans died as a stand collapsed during a game against New South Wales
    b) Lions captain Robert Seddon drowned in the Hunter river
    c) manager Arthur Shrewsbury was shot dead in a Brisbane public house

6. **South Africa lost 16–25 in the first test of the 1997 tour. Who became the most-capped Springbok in the game, with 38 matches under his belt?**

    a) Hennie le Roux
    b) James Small
    c) Mark Andrews

7. **Which Lions international coached Munster to a famous 12–0 victory over the All Blacks in October 1978?**

    a) Ray McLoughlin
    b) Jimmy Nelson
    c) Tom Kiernan

8. **Who were the two scrum halves to make test appearances on the 1966 Lions tour?**

9. **Who, with two touch-downs, was the Lions' top try scorer in the 1980 series against South Africa?**

10. **Which country, with 12 representatives, contributed the most players to the Lions' original 36-man squad to travel to South Africa in 2009?**

Round 45

1. **The 1891 Lions squad consisted of 21 players. How many of them had attended Oxford or Cambridge Universities?**

    a) 14
    b) 16
    c) 21

2. **Who was appointed Head of Communications for the Lions' 2005 tour?**

    a) Alastair Campbell
    b) Karren Brady
    c) Martin Sorrell

3. **Which of the following Welshmen scored the most test points for the Lions?**

    a) Phil Bennett
    b) Neil Jenkins
    c) Stephen Jones

4. **Which hooker failed to make an appearance on the 2001 tour due to a knee injury he picked up during training in Perth?**

    a) Frankie Sheahan
    b) Phil Greening
    c) Robbie Russell

5. **Back-row forward Richard Hill was capped on five occasions by the Lions. How many times did he make an international appearance for England?**

    a) 71
    b) 84
    c) 92

6. **New Zealand narrowly defeated the Lions 20–18 in the first test of the 1993 tour. Who was selected at hooker for the game?**

    a) Brian Moore
    b) Kenny Milne
    c) Steve Smith

7. **What did Carl Aarvold do for the Lions in 1930 that Malcolm Price later did in 1959, and Gerald Davies in 1971?**

    a) scored two tries in a match against New Zealand
    b) started three consecutive tests in three different positions against the All Blacks
    c) kicked two drop goals in a Lions series

8. **Tom Smith and Rob Wainwright were the only two Scotland-based forwards in the 1997 squad. Which club did they both play for?**

9. **Who made a record 17 Lions test appearances between 1962 and 1975?**

10. **Which member of the 1950 touring party reached the semi-final race of the 100 metres at the 1948 Summer Olympic Games?**

Round 46

1. **Which Irishman was dropped for the crucial, series-deciding third test against Australia in 2013?**
   a) Brian O'Driscoll
   b) Paul O'Connell
   c) Tommy Bowe

2. **Clive Woodward was selected as a player for both the 1980 and 1983 tours. How many test appearances did he make?**
   a) 0
   b) 2
   c) 4

3. **Who displaced Will Carling for the last two test matches of the 1993 series?**
   a) Scott Gibbs
   b) Vince Cunningham
   c) Scott Hastings

4. **Blackburn-born Will Greenwood was selected for three Lions tours. What was his first paid job?**
   a) installing tachographs on lorries
   b) talking-books clerk
   c) transcriptionist for surgeons

5. **Who became the first Australia rugby league international to play for the Wallabies, with a rugby union career that included three tests against the 2001 Lions?**

   a) Wendell Sailor

   b) Andrew Walker

   c) Lote Tuqiri

6. **How did Theo Samuels write his name into South Africa rugby history in the second Lions test of the 1896 tour?**

   a) first test match points-scorer for South Africa

   b) first South Africa international to win ten caps

   c) first non-Western Province player to represent South Africa

7. **Finlay Calder holds a unique place in Lions history. What is it?**

   a) the only player whose Lions career solely consisted of test matches, having not made an appearance in a non-test tour game

   b) the only forward to score a try in each game of a test series

   c) the only 20th-century Lions captain to win a series having lost the first match

8. **Who scored 236 points in 27 Lions matches across two tours in 1974 and 1977?**

9. **Dublin-born Nick Popplewell made seven appearances on the 1993 tour. Which club did he play for at the time?**

10. **Which three-times capped Lion was coach of Boroughmuir for nine years from 1986, winning the First Division Championship in 1991?**

Round 47

1. **In which year did Alex Corbisiero, Richie Gray and Simon Zebo make their Lions debut?**

    a) 2005

    b) 2009

    c) 2013

2. **Neath wing Elgan Rees made 19 Lions appearances across two tours in 1977 and 1980. How many tries did he score?**

    a) 7

    b) 9

    c) 11

3. **Which club is associated with Willie John McBride?**

    a) Lisburn

    b) Ballymena

    c) Dungannon

4. **What links Welsh Lions Teddy Morgan, Jack Matthews, J P R Williams and Jamie Roberts?**

    a) all qualified as doctors

    b) all were junior British tennis champions

    c) all represented Wales at the Commonwealth Games

5. In 2016 Lion Lewis Tierney became the first son of a rugby league Super League Grand Final winner to play in and win a Grand Final himself. Name the father.

   a) John Bentley
   b) Alan Tait
   c) Jason Robinson

6. Having played in 20 matches, who made the most appearances during the 1962 tour of South Africa?

   a) Gordon Waddell
   b) Mike Campbell-Lamerton
   c) Niall Brophy

7. New Zealand defeated the Lions 38–6 at Eden Park in July 1983. Who scored a hat trick of tries in the game?

   a) Allan Hewson
   b) Bernie Fraser
   c) Stu Wilson

8. Scotland's Doddie Weir appeared three times on the 1997 Lions tour. Which position did he play?

9. Which Irish hooker was selected for the 1974 Lions tour, eight years after making four test appearances on the 1966 tour?

10. Who were the three players selected for both the 1971 and 1977 Lions tours?

Round 48

1. **How many penalty kicks did Tom Kiernan, Bob Hiller and Stephen Jones score from for the Lions between them?**

    a) 55

    b) 62

    c) 74

2. **Who appeared in the Lions' starting line-up for the first New Zealand test in 2005, two years after making his last appearance for his country?**

    a) Steve Thompson

    b) Jonny Wilkinson

    c) Ben Kay

3. **Who was the youngest member of the 2013 touring party?**

    a) Stuart Hogg

    b) George North

    c) Owen Farrell

4. **During the 1968 tour of South Africa, who became the first person to earn a Lions cap by coming off the bench as a replacement?**

    a) Barry Bresnihan

    b) Sandy Hinshelwood

    c) Mike Gibson

5. **Border lost by four points to the Lions in 1997. Who scored a late try to give the tourists victory?**

   a) Rob Wainwright
   b) Nick Beal
   c) Eric Miller

6. **What was significant about the Lions test match on 12 June 1910?**

   a) first time Argentina awarded a cap in a match
   b) first international match to be played in North America
   c) the only Lions test ever played in Fiji

7. **Chris Oti made his England debut in 1988, becoming the first black player in 80 years to do so. How many times did he wear a Lions jersey on the 1989 tour?**

   a) 2
   b) 3
   c) 5

8. **Who were the three players used on the wing during the 1974 test series?**

9. **Who in 2001 became the first player to represent the Lions in three different decades?**

10. **The Lions lost the 2009 tour series against South Africa, but in the same year three members of the squad were shortlisted for the IRB Player of the Year award. Name them.**

Round 49

1. **In 2015, which Lion received a knighthood in the Queen's birthday honours?**

    a) Gareth Edwards

    b) David Duckham

    c) Barry John

2. **Which of the following players made the most Lions test appearances?**

    a) Dewi Bebb

    b) James Farrell

    c) Fran Cotton

3. **Which club side provided four players from three different countries for the 1924 tour?**

    a) Hawick

    b) Birkenhead Park

    c) Newport

4. **The Lions scored 73 points in the second half of their demolition of a Queensland President's XV side in 2001. Which centre scored a hat trick of tries in the match?**

    a) Will Greenwood

    b) Rob Henderson

    c) Mark Taylor

5. **Austin Healey appeared in an episode of the BBC's *Celebrity Mastermind* in January 2013. What was his specialist subject?**
    a) the career of Tommy Cooper
    b) James Bond – the Roger Moore films
    c) Everton Football Club 1984–1994

6. **Which member of the 1971 Lions team was New Zealand's Colin Meads referring to when he said he 'had us donkey-licked'?**
    a) Mervyn Davies
    b) John Taylor
    c) Willie John McBride

7. **Gerald Kyrke made 11 appearances on the 1908 tour. Which founding-member club of the RFU did he play for?**
    a) Queen's House
    b) Marlborough Nomads
    c) Wimbledon Hornets

8. **Nigel Redman was called into the 1997 touring squad as an injury replacement for Doddie Weir. Which club side did he represent on 350 occasions?**

9. **Name the four Scotland forwards selected for the 1993 tour.**

10. **What role did Wales international Dr John Griffin have in the first ever Lions test match, played in July 1891?**

Round 50

1. **Jonathan Sexton made his Lions debut against the Barbarians in June 2013. Which country did he represent on his test debut against Fiji in November 2009?**

    a) Scotland

    b) England

    c) Ireland

2. **Angus Black, Nigel Melville and Gareth Cooper made a combined 16 Lions appearances. Which position did they all play?**

    a) full back

    b) scrum half

    c) centre

3. **Tom Richards joined the 1910 Lions as a tour replacement. Two years previously he had been an Olympic gold medallist. Which country did he represent in rugby union at the Games?**

    a) Australia

    b) USA

    c) Canada

4. **Who scored three tries in four matches before his 1980 tour came to an end due to a combination of shoulder and knee injuries?**

    a) Bruce Hay

    b) Gareth Davies

    c) Terry Holmes

5. **Which Scotland international won eight caps over three tours in the 1970s?**

   a) Dougie Morgan

   b) Gordon Brown

   c) Billy Steele

6. **Who was the South Africa coach who led his team to a series defeat against the Lions in 1997?**

   a) Carel du Plessis

   b) Nick Mallett

   c) Andre Markgraaff

7. **Brothers Richard, Paul and David Wallace were all selected for Lions squads. Which one made the most tour appearances?**

   a) Richard

   b) Paul

   c) David

8. **Richard Hill was selected for three Lions tours. Which role was he appointed to by the Rugby Football Union in September 2016?**

9. **What happened on 6 July 1904 following Denys Dobson's dismissal against Northern Districts?**

10. **Western Australia lost by 106 points to the Lions in June 2001. Who played out of position at full back for the Lions in the match?**

Answers

Round 1

1. a
2. c
3. b
4. a
5. c
6. a
7. b
8. Nick Farr-Jones
9. Rob Wainwright
10. Roy Kinnear

Round 2

1. a
2. c
3. c
4. a
5. b
6. a
7. b
8. Ieuan Evans, Jeremy Guscott and Dai Young
9. Tony O'Reilly
10. Hooker

Round 3

1. b
2. a
3. b

4. a
5. c
6. b
7. b
8. John Pullin
9. Ben Cohen
10. Gordon Bulloch, Martin Corry, Brian O'Driscoll, Michael Owen and Gareth Thomas

Round 4

1. c
2. c
3. a
4. b
5. c
6. a
7. c
8. Warren Gatland
9. Jeremy Guscott
10. J J Williams

Round 5

1. c
2. b
3. b
4. a
5. c
6. b
7. c
8. Shane Williams
9. Phil Vickery
10. England and Scotland

Round 6

1. a
2. c
3. b
4. b
5. b
6. a
7. c
8. Paul O'Connell
9. teachers
10. Ian McGeechan

Round 7

1. a   (Edwards 61, Healey 25, Andrew 47)
2. b
3. b
4. c
5. a
6. c
7. a
8. John Bentley
9. Reg Skrimshire
10. Mike Slemen

Round 8

1. b   (Bush 5, Rutherford 5, Chalmers 7)
2. a
3. b
4. a
5. c
6. a
7. c

8. Tony Neary
9. Don Clarke
10. Jonathan Sexton

Round 9

1. c (Irvine 34, Jones 15, Hiller 44)
2. b
3. a
4. b
5. a
6. c
7. b
8. Paul Ackford
9. Neil Jenkins
10. Phil Vickery

Round 10

1. b (Llewellyn 4, Butterfield 3, Tait 1)
2. a
3. c
4. c
5. b
6. a
7. c
8. Frank Laidlaw
9. Duncan McRae
10. Ieuan Evans

Round 11

1. c
2. a
3. b

Answers

4. a
5. c
6. b
7. a
8. Alun Wyn Jones
9. three
10. Euan Murray

Round 12

1. b
2. c
3. a
4. b
5. c
6. a
7. c
8. Jason Robinson, Josh Lewsey and Geordan Murphy
9. two
10. Tom Richards (who played for both Australia and the Lions)

Round 13

1. b (Wilkinson 116, Campbell 184, Waddell 41)
2. a
3. b
4. c
5. a
6. a
7. c
8. David Duckham
9. Mike Weston
10. Neil Back, Lawrence Dallaglio, Matt Dawson, Will Greenwood, Richard Hill and Martin Johnson

Round 14

1. b
2. a
3. c
4. c
5. b
6. c
7. b
8. France
9. Ollie Smith (England)
10. Graham Price

Round 15

1. a
2. c
3. b
4. a
5. a
6. c
7. a (Murphy 41, Nelson 16, Mulligan 22)
8. Andy Irvine
9. Dean Richards
10. Bath

Round 16

1. b
2. c
3. a
4. c
5. b
6. b
7. c

8. 1997 tour of South Africa
9. Gordon Bulloch and Tom Smith
10. Wasps

Round 17

1. a
2. a
3. c
4. c
5. b
6. b
7. c
8. 1997 and 2005
9. Jeremy Davidson
10. Mike Campbell-Lamerton

Round 18

1. a
2. a
3. b
4. c
5. a
6. c
7. a
8. Robin McBryde
9. Willie Duggan
10. Leicester Tigers

Round 19

1. c
2. a
3. a

4. b
5. c
6. b
7. c
8. Tane Norton
9. Martin Johnson
10. Swansea

Round 20

1. a
2. c
3. a
4. a
5. b
6. b
7. c
8. Argentina, New Zealand and South Africa
9. once, in 2005
10. Barry Williams

Round 21

1. b
2. a
3. c
4. c
5. a
6. b
7. c
8. Barry John
9. Israel Folau
10. Bill Beaumont

Round 22

1. c
2. a
3. c
4. b
5. c
6. a
7. c
8. Bakkies Botha
9. Mervyn Davies
10. Northampton

Round 23

1. a
2. b (Iain Balshaw and Matt Perry)
3. c
4. b
5. c
6. a (three)
7. c
8. Leigh Halfpenny
9. Martin Corry
10. Dwayne Peel

Round 24

1. c
2. a
3. a
4. b
5. c
6. c
7. a

8. Allan Bateman
9. Tom Kiernan
10. Bleddyn Williams

Round 25

1. b
2. c
3. a
4. a
5. c
6. b
7. b
8. Sale Sharks
9. Gordon Brown
10. Ian Stephens

Round 26

1. b
2. a
3. c
4. b
5. c
6. c
7. b
8. Chris Oti
9. Graham Price
10. Gareth Edwards, Roger Young and Gordon Connell

Round 27

1. b
2. a
3. b (Davies 107, Gibson 124, Stimpson 111)

4. a
5. b
6. c
7. c
8. Shane Williams
9. Jason White
10. policeman

Round 28

1. a
2. b
3. c (Hayes 5, Grewcock 5, Jenkins 7)
4. a
5. a
6. c
7. a
8. Graham Rowntree
9. Wales
10. Herbert and Gordon Waddell

Round 29

1. c
2. b (Jenkins 27, O'Gara 32, Hastings 15)
3. a
4. b
5. b
6. c
7. a
8. Harlequins
9. Tana Umaga
10. The Scottish and Irish unions refused to permit their players to join the tour, due to their fight against professionalism and the Northern Union.

Round 30

1. a
2. c
3. c
4. b
5. b
6. a
7. c
8. Scarlets
9. David Duckham
10. Howard Norris

Round 31

1. b
2. a
3. c
4. b
5. a
6. c
7. b
8. four
9. Harry Ellis
10. They won a silver medal at the Olympic Games in rugby union.

Round 32

1. a
2. a
3. b (Dawson 36, Watkins 43, Chalmers 28)
4. b
5. c
6. b

7. b
8. Sid Going
9. Jim (1983) and Finlay (1989) Calder
10. more – 9 tries from 14 matches

Round 33

1. a
2. c
3. a
4. c
5. b
6. a
7. a
8. Gethin Jenkins
9. Ulster
10. Syd Millar

Round 34

1. a
2. c
3. a
4. c
5. a
6. b
7. a
8. Ronnie Dawson
9. Bay of Plenty
10. Graham Price and Jeff Squire

Round 35

1. c
2. a

3. a
4. c
5. c
6. b
7. c
8. Dave Alred
9. Rob Henderson
10. the trial of Reggie and Ronnie Kray

Round 36

1. b
2. c
3. a
4. c
5. a (penalty and conversion)
6. a
7. c
8. Wasps
9. Dorian West
10. Willie John McBride

Round 37

1. b
2. b
3. a
4. b
5. c
6. c
7. c
8. Ross Ford
9. Mark Regan
10. Edward and William Bromet

Round 38

1. a (Irvine 20, Jackson 19, Smith 17)
2. a
3. c
4. b
5. a
6. c
7. c
8. John Dawes
9. Shane Williams
10. one, in 1989

Round 39

1. b
2. b
3. a
4. c
5. c
6. b
7. a
8. Leigh Halfpenny
9. Bill Beaumont
10. Syd Millar

Round 40

1. a
2. c
3. a (McLauchlan 8, Carmichael 0, Sole 3)
4. c
5. b
6. b
7. a

8. John Eales
9. Hugh McLeod
10. Bev Risman (son of Gus Risman)

Round 41

1. b
2. a
3. a
4. c
5. c
6. b
7. a
8. Barry John
9. Mike Catt, Mark Regan and Simon Shaw
10. Gordon Bulloch

Round 42

1. b
2. b (Wade 1, Barritt 2, Williams 1)
3. b
4. a
5. c
6. c
7. a
8. Gavin Hastings
9. Ray Gravell
10. Simon Easterby

Round 43

1. a
2. b
3. b

4. b
5. b
6. c
7. c
8. Paul O'Connell, Jamie Heaslip, Mike Phillips and Stephen Jones
9. Alexander Obolensky
10. yes (Hare (6), Hastings (18) and Perry (6) made 30 appearances between them. Williams made 29 appearances.)

Round 44

1. a
2. b
3. a
4. c
5. b
6. b
7. c
8. Allan Lewis and Roger Young
9. John O'Driscoll
10. Wales

Round 45

1. b (14 Cambridge, 2 Oxford)
2. a
3. c (Bennett 44, Jenkins 41, Jones 53)
4. b
5. a
6. b
7. a
8. Watsonians

9. Willie John McBride
10. Ken Jones

Round 46

1. a
2. b
3. a
4. a
5. b
6. a
7. c
8. Phil Bennett
9. Greystones
10. Bruce Hay

Round 47

1. c
2. c
3. b
4. a
5. c
6. b
7. c
8. second row
9. Ken Kennedy
10. Gordon Brown, Mike Gibson and Derek Quinnell

Round 48

1. c (Kiernan 22, Hiller 34, Jones 18)
2. b
3. a
4. c

5. a
6. a
7. b
8. Andy Irvine, Billy Steele and J J Williams
9. Dai Young
10. Tom Croft, Jamie Heaslip and Brian O'Driscoll

Round 49

1. a
2. a (Bebb 8, Farrell 5, Cotton 7)
3. c (Harold Davies, Wales; Vince Griffiths, Wales; Neil McPherson, Scotland; William Roche, Ireland)
4. b
5. c
6. a
7. b
8. Bath
9. Paul Burnell, Damian Cronin, Kenny Milne and Peter Wright
10. He was the referee.

Round 50

1. c
2. b
3. a
4. c
5. b
6. a
7. c (Richard 5, Paul 6, David 9)
8. England rugby team manager
9. Captain David Bedell-Sivright marched his men off the field in protest. The Lions returned 20 minutes later to win the match 17–3.
10. Brian O'Driscoll

THE RUGBY UNION QUIZ BOOK

TEST YOUR KNOWLEDGE ON WORLD RUGBY

MATTHEW JONES

y Lolfa

£3.99

So you think you know Welsh rugby?

Welsh Rugby QUIZ

Matthew Jones   y Lolfa

£3.95

The Six Nations Rugby Quiz Book

Matthew Jones   y Lolfa

£3.95

The Lions Rugby Quiz Book is just
one of a whole range of publications from
Y Lolfa. For a full list of books currently in print,
send now for your free copy of our new full-
colour catalogue. Or simply surf into our website

www.ylolfa.com

for secure on-line ordering.

TALYBONT CEREDIGION CYMRU SY24 5HE
e-mail ylolfa@ylolfa.com
website www.ylolfa.com
phone (01970) 832 304
fax 832 782